# Nature Explorer

## GET OUTSIDE, OBSERVE, AND DISCOVER THE NATURAL WORLD

Jenny deFouw Geuder

PUBLICATIONS
Adventure
an imprint of Adventure**KEEN**

## ABOUT THE AUTHOR

**Jenny deFouw Geuder** is an artist and educator from Michigan. She received her bachelor's and master's degrees in art education (and minored in English). She has taught art at the middle-school level for 16 years and has continued her own artistic interests on the side, both in commissioned work and personal topics. She primarily works in watercolor, but she also enjoys oils, ceramics, and graphite. She lives in the country with her husband, two small boys, a dog, five cats, a hedgehog, chickens, and occasionally two ponies.

Cover and book design by Jonathan Norberg

Edited by Brett Ortler

Proofread by Ritchey Halphen

Photo Credits:
Author photo © 2023 by Josh Knap/Peninsula Photography

Reference images for the following watercolors:
**Jeffrey Hamilton/Unsplash.com:** 10; **Brett Ortler:** 114 (bottom right), 115 (top left); **Peninsula Photography:** 17; **WisconsinPollinators.com:** 107 (Bumblebee); Ming H Yao: back cover (Sandhill Crane and baby).

Activities on the following pages were inspired by the following websites:
**ChurchStreetDesigns.com:** 108-109; **FrugalFun4Boys.com:** 70-71; **GrowingaJeweledRose.com:** 40-41.

*reference image credits  continued on page 136*

10 9 8 7 6 5 4 3 2 1

**Nature Explorer: Get Outside, Observe, and Discover the Natural World**

Copyright © 2023 by Jenny deFouw Geuder
Published by Adventure Publications
An imprint of AdventureKEEN
310 Garfield Street South
Cambridge, Minnesota 55008
(800) 678-7006
www.adventurepublications.net
All rights reserved
Printed in China
Cataloging-in-Publication Data is available from the Library of Congress
ISBN 978-1-64755-347-0 (pbk.); ISBN 978-1-64755-348-7 (ebook)

**Dedication**
To Evan and Henry:
I love you to the moon and back...now go outside.

# Table of Contents

# What Is a Naturalist?

A naturalist is someone who looks closely at nature: plants, animals, insects, fossils, and more. Kids are drawn to nature and quick to investigate their world, it's in their "nature"! So go outside, explore, and look closer. Ask questions about what you see. Write down or sketch what you see. Go for walks, and look around, down by your feet, and up in the tree branches.

# HOW TO BE A NATURALIST

One of the most important parts about being a naturalist is the simplest: Record your observations. By writing down **what**, **when** and **where** you observe something, you're creating a record for your area, and that's useful to scientists today—and in the future.

Journaling Tips:
- Keep a notebook! Write down the things you see, and when.
- Try to identify things you find (there are lots of websites and apps for that; see page 133). If you can't figure exactly what is, that's fine, but try to narrow it down as much as you can.
- Sketch the things you like the most.
- Look close! What do you notice? Look, then look again. Notice textures, angles. Simplify things to basic shapes and add details later.
- Ask questions, and write down what you find out later.

A Recommended Gear List (Not Necessary, but Nice!):
- sketchbook
- pencils/pens
- camera
- watercolor/colored pencils
- binoculars
- magnifying glass
- water
- backpack
- compass

actual size

## STAY SAFE!

When you head outside, don't go alone, and make sure a parent/guardian knows where you are and when you left. Better yet, have an adult go with you, and bring a cell phone for emergencies.

Check the weather before you go for a hike, and be prepared for a change in the weather. And don't forget sunscreen and bug spray!

Let wild plants and animals stay wild. Don't eat anything you find, and keep your distance from animals when observing them.

Know the potentially dangerous plants and critters in your area. For example, Poison Ivy is really common throughout much of the country and gives a bad rash! You might know the phrase "Leaves of three, leave them be," so watch out for plants with compound leaves with three leaflets (the middle one the longest). If you accidentally touch a "problem plant," wash the area really well right away with soap and water.

Use bug spray, wear long pants, and do a good wood tick check when you get home. If you find a tick attached to your body, have a parent help you remove it as soon as possible, and follow up with a doctor if need be. Ticks can be really small!

## LOOK CLOSE, WAIT, AND BE QUIET

The first step in being a naturalist is simple: slow down and watch nature. Take your time! Let nature "come awake" around you. Try staying very still for a few minutes and see what you see and hear. Look closer at things: Be curious! Notice things and be patient.

"In every walk with Nature one receives far more than they seek." John Muir, *Mormon Lilies*, 1870

# Use Your Senses to Experience Your World!

One of the best ways to learn about the nature near you is simple: Use your senses! By focusing on specific senses—hearing, smell, and touch— you can focus your attention and discover things you might have otherwise missed!

## HEARING

Close your eyes and sit quietly. Try to identify what you hear. Is it a bird? A frog? A cricket? Write down what you hear, and then close your eyes again and sit a little longer. What else do you hear? Do you hear the wind rustling the leaves, birds chirping, or something else? Can you hear more than one type of bird call?

**Did You Know?** Human ears include three tiny muscles and the three smallest bones in our bodies, but compared to ours, animal ears are really impressive. For example, cats have far more muscles than we do—and they can move theirs toward sound, birds can pinpoint sounds from long distances away, and bats can even hear ultrasound—sounds human ears can't even detect!

## SMELL

Close your eyes and this time focus on what you *smell*. Depending on where you are, you might smell many different things! Can you smell rain? Wet dirt? Hot pavement? A pine tree? Maybe you can smell cut grass or flowers. Explore your space and use your sense of smell—pinch a leaf of a plant you know is safe, and smell it. Some smell great (sassafras, pine needles), but some smell bitter. What smells are your favorite? Your sense of smell is often linked to your memories: Do the things you smell remind you of anything or a memory you have?

**Did you Know?** Humans have a pretty good sense of smell, but some animals have one that's much better. Dogs are famous for their good sense of smell, and some kinds of dogs—bloodhounds, for example—have a sense of smell hundreds of times better than ours. But bears probably have the best sense of smell of all. They can smell food from huge distances away!

## TOUCH

Sit quietly with your eyes closed, and reach out with your fingers: What do you feel? Crunchy grass? Soft moss? Warm pavement or rocks? Maybe the soft velvet of sand? Explore your space with your fingers—but stick to plants and animals you know are safe to touch. Touch tree bark and notice which bark is rough, and which is smooth. Touch the soft moss, and the crackly dry leaves. Feel a hard rock or a fuzzy dandelion. Write down your observations. What things feel "nice" or comforting, and which don't you like?

**Did You Know?**

Your sense of touch is one of the first senses you use. From birth, babies instinctively wrap their hands around their parents' fingers. (It takes a lot longer for a baby's eyes to work like an adult's.) Animals rely on their sense of touch too: Whiskers on mammals, such as cats and dogs, help them notice very slight movements, such as the direction of the wind. Birds are sensitive to the lightest touch of their feathers too; they have touch receptors at the base of their feathers. Some also have special feathers near their beaks that they "touch" with as well!

"Humankind has not woven the web of life. We are but one thread within it. Whatever we do to the web, we do to ourselves. All things are bound together. All things connect." Chief Seattle, 1854

## SIGHT: LOOKING CLOSER

Sit quietly and let yourself relax. Watch nature around you and write down what you see. But most importantly, stay there awhile—we tend to notice big movements first, but when we give ourselves time to sit and look, we start to notice the smaller stuff! And nature starts to relax around us and comes out to play. So look down by your feet. Lean in and look, there's a whole world happening! Look for ants, mushrooms, tiny bugs, spiders, and more. Then lean back and look up into the tops of the branches: Some birds prefer to stay up in the canopy. What colors do you see? Textures? New things you didn't see before?

**Did You Know?** Some birds, such as eagles and falcons, have eyes that are much larger than ours (proportionally speaking), and they see clearly from a great distance, maybe even a mile away. They can also focus their vision on more than one thing at one time, which is helpful as they hunt.

Use the sun to capture cool plant silhouettes! Also known as cyanotypes (sigh-an-oh-types), they have been around for two hundred years, and they are really fun to do. When sunlight interacts with a special paper, it changes the color of the visible paper and leaves the silhouette of any objects on the paper behind.

### WHAT YOU'LL NEED

Plants, flowers, leaves

Cyanotype paper (available online or at craft stores, look for a Sun Art kit)

Clear acrylic/plexiglass sheet (if you get a kit, it is usually included)

A tub of water or a sink

Lemon juice (optional)

18

1. Go explore! Find fun, flat objects out in nature. Consider choosing flowers of different shapes, leaves with neat edges, and so on.

2. In the shade, arrange your plants and flowers on the paper. Only the silhouettes will be visible! You might find it helpful to put the special paper on a piece of cardboard to keep it steady.

3. Carefully set the clear sheet on top. This isn't necessary, but it keeps things from blowing away or shifting as you carry your paper. If things aren't close to the paper, the image will turn out more "ghostly" or soft edged.

4. Then, place the paper in direct sunlight for 5–10 minutes (see directions on package). It should turn very pale or white in color.

5. Set the paper into the tub of water and rinse it for about one minute. If you'd like a deeper shade of blue, add some drops of lemon juice. The colors on your page should shift and invert; the silhouettes should be bright white and the background deep cyan blue!

6. Set your paper out on a towel flat to dry or hang from a string somewhere dark or out of the sun.

Experiment with different shapes! Try feathers, flowers, leaves, grass. What if you arrange them like a wreath, or more like a bouquet? Which plants' silhouettes are the most interesting?

Sun prints work on fabric too!

# Make Your Own Prism

Use a mirror and water to break white light into all the colors of the rainbow! Visible light is white, and it contains all the other colors. The different wavelengths of light correspond to individual colors. In everyday life, we see objects as specific colors because they absorb some wavelengths of light and reflect others back to us. (A red apple, for example, reflects red light back to our eyes.)

The longest wavelengths create what we see as red, while the shortest ones create what we see as violet. There are also wavelengths of light our eyes can't see—for example, ultraviolet and infrared!

Try this experiment to break white light into the full spectrum of colors (a rainbow).

## WHAT YOU'LL NEED

A clear water glass

Water

A small mirror

White paper

**1** Fill a glass with water, and then set it by a window with bright sunlight.

**2** Hold the mirror in your hand and catch the sunlight with it, and then direct through the glass. You should see a rainbow. (This might take a little trial and error if it doesn't work right way.)

**3** Place your piece of paper where the rainbow just was, then hold the mirror the same way again. The rainbow should be easy to see on the paper!

**Fun Fact:**
Most humans can distinguish about a million different colors.

# Habitats

Another way to get to know the nature near you is to learn about all the various types of habitats that exist. From a backyard and local green spaces to something as simple as an empty lot, nature is everywhere! Of course, you should be familiar with the potentially dangerous critters in your area before you go out exploring.

## BACKYARDS

A backyard is a great place to start exploring nature! Grab your binoculars and spend some time learning about what creatures call your backyard home. You might see goldfinches, Mourning Doves, Blue Jays, robins, or hummingbirds, especially if you put up bird feeders. Squirrels, chipmunks, and even skunks and raccoons don't mind living near homes. But look closer to see the butterflies and bees coming to your flowers, the tiny beetles, pillbugs, and snails living in a little world right outside your door.

## WETLANDS, RIVERS, AND LAKES

Many different animals are drawn to water. Herons, plover, loons, ducks, eagles, and kingfishers can be found living near the water's edge. You might be lucky enough to see a watersnake, a turtle, a newt or salamander, a beaver or muskrat, or even an alligator if you're in the southern U.S. Look for the unique water-loving insects too: dragonflies, whirligigs, and water skaters.

## EMPTY LOTS

At first glance, you might not think to find nature in that empty lot near your home, but look again! Wild things can live in all sorts of places, even in heavily developed urban areas. Pigeons, Blue Jays, raccoons, rabbits, and squirrels are everywhere, but also look for butterflies and bees, beetles, and ants. Many major cities are now home to Peregrine Falcons as well! Weeds and wildflowers are also quick to grow wherever there is space too!

## PARKS

Parks contain a lot of biodiversity (that means a wide range of animals, plants, and other life)! Spend some time walking around the trails at your local park and see who lives there. You might see Red-Shouldered Hawks, woodpeckers, Barred Owls, herons, deer, skunk, and bats! Turtles, snakes, and a whole bunch of other creatures and bugs can sometimes be found at your local park.

## FORESTS

Woodland creatures like the shelter and safety that trees provide, and they often tend to be skittish and run away when spooked. Spend some time sitting quietly to see more! Animals such as porcupines, opossums, White-Tailed Deer, foxes, rabbits, chipmunks and squirrels all call the forest their home. Some birds that love the forest are woodpeckers, owls, nuthatches, flickers, and chickadees. You also might see pine, maple, beech, and oak trees, as well as neat plants like bracken ferns.

## DESERTS AND DRY AREAS

Finding and using water is the top priority in desert areas. Many of the plants and animals have specific adaptations that help them survive. That's why you'll find unique plants like cacti, the yucca, sagebrush, saltbush, and wildflowers such as penstemon, a hummingbird favorite. Animals that you might spot include prairie dogs, Bighorn Sheep, jackrabbits, roadrunners, and even critters such as rattlesnakes, scorpions, Gila Monsters, and Javelinas. To stay safe, avoid putting your hands where you can't see, keep your distance from potentially dangerous critters, and don't pick up wild animals. Instead, enjoy a sighting, from a distance!

# Make a Fairy Garden or a Toad House

Fairy gardens are a fun way to turn natural objects into art. Make your own fantasy house for a forest friend! If fairies aren't your thing, you can also make a toad house, also known as a "toad abode." (Abode's another word for house.) The materials you'll need for both are the same.

## WHAT YOU'LL NEED

A clay pot

Two plates or trays to hold your pots

A hot glue gun (use with an adult's help)

Natural materials: small rocks, sticks, grass, acorns, pinecones, moss

**1** Start out by finding a good location (a backyard or another area where you have permission to be) is good. If you are making a fairy house, you can use your garden space or a large pot or tray.

**2** If you want to attract a toad (they are wonderful garden guests who eat a ton of bugs and are fun to see), look for a shady place, perhaps under a shrub or bush. Being closer to a water source is helpful, but you can set one of the clay pots into the ground as a "pool."

**3** With an adult's help, chip out a hole about two inches across in the edge of the pot. This will be a door. Then, take the flowerpot and turn it upside down. Place it on the tray/plates. Make a roof using the pot's drainage tray on top! Then it's time to decorate: look around for natural materials. You can glue pebbles and rocks to the outside, twigs, and pinecones can look like shingles. Hot glue works the best, but make sure you use it safely. You can add dirt and press moss onto the roof to make a living roof too; the moss can grow and spread around your fairy house.

**4** If you're making a toad house, place your house around your yard or garden. Check the water pool regularly to make sure it doesn't go dry. You can tuck some leaves into the house for your toad friend to burrow in.

## Terrarium: How to Make Your Own Mini Habitat!

A terrarium is a mini garden in a glass bowl (either completely closed or open at the top). It lets heat and light in, but keeps the moisture in, like a tiny ecosystem. (In fact, that's where terrariums get their name; *terra* means "earth.")

## WHAT YOU'LL NEED

A glass container with no drainage holes, with or without a top; if you have one with a top, it should be airtight

Small plants

Clean aquarium gravel or small crushed stone

Activated charcoal (found at nurseries or pet supply stores; look in the fish supplies section)

Clean potting soil mix

Moss

Little plastic animals/fairy garden pieces (if wanted)

**1** First, choose your container. A jar with a wide enough mouth to fit your hand is best. (*Tip*: Open containers are less likely to get mold, but they are open to the air, so they will dry out quickly and are best suited for succulents and other plants that don't need a lot of water.) Then choose your plants. You can use almost any small plants, but a good idea is to keep plants together that need the same water amounts. Succulents, violets, moss, and tropical plants do well in terrariums.

**2** Then layer your drainage materials on the bottom of your pot:

On the bottom, use your crushed gravel. Then add some activated charcoal (helps with drainage and keeps smells away). Next, add a little layer of sheet moss. Finally, add in potting soil mix. Save room for your plants! Now add your plants! Plan ahead for different heights for your plants. Now: Decorate! Add any rocks, plastic animals, or other decorations.

**3** Water carefully, just enough to get it damp, not soaked. Terrariums don't need a lot of water, check it every now and then to see if the soil is dry. If you get a lot of condensation inside, open the lid to dry it out a little.

Goldenrod

Common
Milkweed

Black-Eyed
Susan

Trillium

Spiderwort

"Many eyes go through the meadow,
but few see the flowers in it."

Ralph Waldo Emerson, 1834

# Flowers

Hairy Puccoon

Western Sunflower

Cardinal Flower

Bellflower

Wild Bergamot

Daisy Fleabane

Chicory

Dandelion

White Clover

Broadleafed Dock

Purple Deadnettle

Blue Violet

34

Lanceleaf
Coreopsis

White
Yarrow

Daisy

Queen Anne's
Lace

St. John's
Wort

## Common "Weeds"

What wildflowers do you have around your yard? Can you find beauty in weeds others might walk right by?

"Weeds are wildflowers, too, once you get to know them."

Unknown

White Pine

White Oak

Balsam Fir

Pawpaw

Bunchberry

Mulberry

Crabapple

# Common Trees

What trees do you know? Go explore and record how many different types of trees you have in your backyard or a park. Are some similar? Pine and fir tree leaves look more like needles, and most leaves stay all year. Most deciduous trees lose their leaves in the fall; before they do, the leaves turn amazing colors.

Sugar Maple

Beech

Birch

Dogwood

Sassafras

Red Oak

Aspen

Capture the beauty of a leaf and keep forever! This simple craft is a good way to record the leaves you find, as well as an easy way to learn more about the parts of a leaf.

### WHAT YOU'LL NEED

Leaves

Paper (thin copy paper works better than thick cardstock)

Crayons or oil pastels (crayons that have lost their paper jackets work the best!)

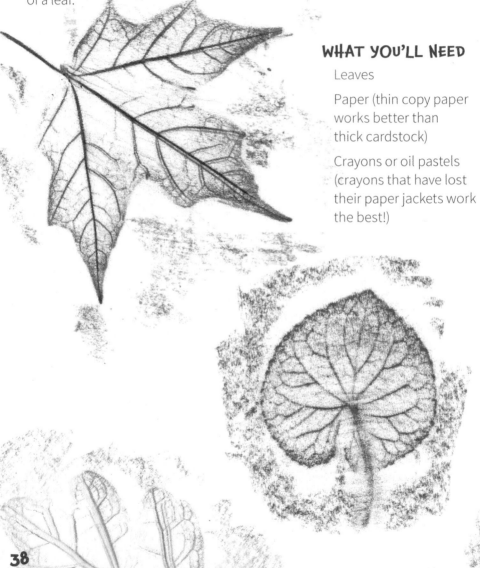

## WHAT TO DO

1. Gather up a variety of leaves. The flatter the leaf, the easier it will be to color over.

2. Lay the leaf facedown on the table, so the veins of the leaf are up.

3. Set the paper over the leaves.

4. Rub the crayon over the covered leaf. You can put the crayon horizontally to color smoothly.

## TAKE IT FURTHER

Try layering two different colors.

What happens if you watercolor over your crayon rubbings? Try a warmly colored paint over a cool-color crayon (or the other way around). For example, try painting a yellow paint over a green crayon rubbing. Warm colors are red, orange, and yellow. Cool colors are blue, green, and purple.

Try colored pencils or graphite pencil.

Try other things besides leaves, like flowers.

Try wax paper or parchment paper for a different look.

Record your leaves in a sketchbook and label them. Once you're done, you'll have made your own tree identification book! Make notes about where you found the leaf or tree, and observations about the bark appearance too!

## Leaf Animals

In the fall, when there are leaves all around, why not use some to make some fun art?

### WHAT YOU'LL NEED

Leaves! Collect different colors, sizes, and shapes. Find anything else natural that might be interesting: grass, acorns, small rocks.

A heavy book

Plastic googly eyes (available at crafts stores)

Glue (optional)

Paper

Construction paper (optional)

1 First, flatten your leaves. Set them under a heavy book for a week to flatten.

2 After the leaves are flat, lay out your materials in front of you, and get creative! Use leaves to make animal bodies, heads, ears. You can use a marker to add features or googly eyes.

3 Once you have them the way you want them, glue them together, or to the construction paper.

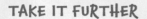

## TAKE IT FURTHER

Create a whole scene for your creature: a house, a "tree," the ground, all out of leaves!

To make a hedgehog, cut a teardrop shape about 5–6" across out of tan construction paper. Draw a face with markers or add googly eyes. Arrange spiky leaves like maple leaves across the hedgehog's back, layering from the back to the front.

Can you write a story about one of your leaf animals?

41

# Land Art

What is land art? Land art is created by artists who use natural materials to create art that is meant to be temporary, often recording it only with a photo before letting it disappear back into nature. The most notable land artist right now is Andy Goldsworthy. He is an English artist who uses ice, leaves, rocks, and anything else he finds in the wild to create amazing sculptures. His work is 100 percent natural—he doesn't use glue or string—just ice, water, mud, gravity to hold things together. Look up some of his work, and then try to make some of your own!

## WHAT YOU'LL NEED

Anything natural! Leaves, rocks, sticks, dirt, and the like. Gather anything that looks interesting to you. Try not to disrupt too much of how the space looked before you. Land art should look natural.

The right space: A flat bit of ground? The roots of a tree? Where would your piece look best?

Note: Only make land art where you have permission to do so. Don't make land art at public parks. Let those places stay wild.

Start arranging! You can stack things, or lay them next to each other. Please, if you stack stones, return them to where you found them! And don't remove rocks from the water's edge—small fish and other creatures often need rocks on the water's edge for protection and for raising their young.

If you need help on coming up with an idea, try a mandala: a mandala is a circular design with radial symmetry. That means things repeat around a central point, like a daisy's petals around the center of the flower.

1. Gently trace a plus sign on the dirt to help you line up your items

2. Place one of your found treasures in the middle: a flower, rock, or leaf.

3. Arrange your objects around that center in circles. Try to set your leaves/objects either on the lines, or halfway between them. That will keep your design lined up straight.

4. Try layering objects, such as a flower over a leaf. Whatever you do on one part of your design, make sure you repeat it around the circle.

## TIPS

Avoid windy days! You will just get frustrated.

Take a picture when you get it done to record it!

Disperse your materials when you are done to help return things to their natural state.

Don't pick flowers or move rocks at parks, especially not at state parks or national parks!

Circles and spirals occur a lot in nature: Try to use some in your art!

# Pressed Flowers and Flower Bookmarks

Flower pressing is a fun craft that people have been enjoying for hundreds of years. This is a great way to preserve some of your lovely treasures. There are two basic options here: You can press flowers in a book or capture your flowers in parchment to enjoy for years to come. There are many ways to preserve flowers!

## PRESSED FLOWERS: WHAT YOU'LL NEED

Heavy book(s)

Paper to absorb moisture (like parchment paper)

Flowers and leaves

1 Open your book, and place parchment paper inside.

2 Arrange your flowers between two pieces of parchment paper (you can fold the paper in half like a book). Try to use flowers of similar size or weight. Leave spaces between different flowers.

3 Carefully close the book. Set a weight (or other books) on top. Leave the weights on top for 2–4 weeks; in the meantime, the flowers will dry.

4 Carefully remove your fragile, dry flowers. You can frame them, put them in a clear phone case, use them on top of gifts instead of a bow or tag, or glue them to paper. Some people use them in cooking (only if an adult checks to make sure it is edible), cleaning, or potpourri (dried flowers and scented oil decorations). Pressed flowers are fragile unless framed, so handle carefully!

## PRESSED FLOWERS BOOKMARK: WHAT YOU'LL NEED

Ironing board and iron

Flowers and leaves

Wax paper

A towel or sheet

**1** On your ironing board, arrange your flowers between two pieces of wax paper. If you want to make bookmarks, make sure you place them in narrow arrangements.

**2** Place a towel or sheet over the wax paper (this keeps the melted wax from getting on your iron)

**3** With an adult, iron the flowers on a low-to-medium setting.

**4** After it is cool, trim to the size and shape you want.

You can trim it to the bookmark size, hole punch the top and run a ribbon hrough it. Or, tape it to a window for a beautiful window suncatcher. You can arrange your flowers in a wreath shape and use it as a picture frame. Parchment ironed flowers will last for years!

## TIPS

Pick your flowers at their peak, with no black marks, and pick them in morning to avoid the dew.

Some flowers keep their color better. Look for ones with thin petals. Thick-petaled flowers or ones that seem "wet" sometimes get moldy or just turn brown.

Flat-faced flowers, like pansies or daisies, flatten the best.

# Flower and Fern Prints

Here's a colorful and fun way to use your flowers!
Make a beautiful bouquet that lasts forever!

## WHAT YOU'LL NEED

Flowers: Those with sturdy stems and petals work best!

Paper/plastic-covered work surface

Craft paint (acrylic or tempera)

A wide, flat painting palette or paper plates

Brushes

Paper

**1** Find lots of great flowers, ferns, and leaves.

**2** Cover your work surface! Squeeze out your paint colors (a quarter-size amount is plenty) on your palette or plate, and spread the paint out a bit so the flower will touch paint . You can add a little water to thin it if it is too thick.

**3** You can either dip your flower directly into the paint, or use the paintbrush to "paint" your flower. I found just dipping the flower to be fun! But for the fern and leaves, I painted it to get better coverage.

**4** Gently press your flower onto your paper, and repeat. You can get several flower "prints" before needing to repaint. For a long fern, you might need to set it down slowly, starting at one end.

## TAKE IT FURTHER

Use construction paper to make cutout "vases" for your flowers! Decorate with markers or paint.

Add stems, ribbons, or leaves with crayons or markers to add more to your picture.

Create your own wrapping paper; use brown craft paper and print flowers all over.

Use leaves and fall color paint to create a fall masterpiece.

Experiment with other things to "print": fingerprints, acorn caps, pine needle bunches, and more!

# NATURE Color

Try a scavenger hunt in nature! Look around you, and try to find objects in nature that match the colors on the color wheel shown here. You can mark the ones you find with a stone or clothespin, or you can set the object right on this book. Everything should be natural: no trash or things made by people!

Look closely! Some colors are harder to find than others!

## TAKE IT FURTHER

Make it a game with another friend!
Who can find their colors first?

For more of a challenge, try doing
the color wheel with insects only, or
plants only, etc. Don't move or harm
the insects—just do a visual comparison!
Handling insects can be harmful to them
(or you!).

# Backyard Birds

**Northern Cardinal—**
An easy-to-spot bird, the male Northern Cardinal actually gets his coloring from the food he eats. Their beaks are short and cone shaped to help them eat seeds.

**Black-Capped Chickadee—**
A common birdfeeder visitor who loves to take seeds and hide them: they can remember where they've hidden food for up to a month! In the winter, they fluff up their feathers to stay warm. Their call, "Chick-a-dee-dee-dee" is recognizable, but the louder/ longer the "dee-dee-dee" in their call, the more they feel threatened.

**Tufted Titmouse—**
A cheerful little bird whose feathers look a little like a party hat! The male and female look alike.

**Rose-Breasted Grosbeak—**
A member of the cardinal family. They sing beautifully, and the female chooses the male based on what song she likes best. They are very territorial.

**Baltimore Oriole**—Bright orange birds that love oranges and jelly! Their nests are woven sock-like sacks that hang from a tree branch.

**Eastern Bluebird**—A beautiful bird with a beautiful song: A male can sing hundreds of songs an hour when trying to attract a mate! You won't get one at your feeder, unless you offer mealworms.

**Ruby-Throated Hummingbird**— Tiny but fierce little birds that love to drink nectar. They can flap their wings 10–15 times per second and can hover and fly backwards. Their nests are about an inch across.

**American Goldfinch**—Males are bright yellow and black in the summer, but turn a bit more olive green in the winter.

**American Crow—**
Some of the smartest birds in the world, crows have amazing memories and can even use tools.

**Mourning Dove—**Their call is a sad-sounding coo (you might mistake it for an owl), and they mate for life. When they eat at a feeder, they can "store" food in their crop, kind of like an extra pouch in their throat, to digest later.

**Dark-Eyed Junco**—Sometimes called a snowbird (since their migration seems to bring cold weather with them), they actually grow a down jacket in the winter, increasing their feathers by 30 percent! They spend their summers in the far north of Canada, but they spend their winters in much of the U.S., including such "warmer" places like Minnesota and Michigan.

**Blue Jay**—A noisy bird at the feeder, blue jays love peanuts the most. Like all blue birds, they aren't actually blue! Their feathers don't have any blue pigment; instead, their feathers scatter light in a way that makes their feathers look blue. When the feathers are backlit (lit from behind), the feathers look brown.

**Northern Flicker—** These woodpeckers love ants! There are two types: the red-shafted and the yellow-shafted. Look for their namesake colors on their wing feathers and head patches.

**Did You Know?** A bird's eye can take up to 15 percent of its head. In a few species, the eyes are bigger than the actual brain! If human eyes were the proportions of those of birds, our eyes would need to be the size of baseballs.

**Red-Headed Woodpecker—** A very striking bird with big black, white and red patches; while flying they look like a checkerboard!

**Red-Bellied Woodpecker**—
It really has more of a red cap
than much of a red belly, but
it has very cool black and
white stripes on its back.
A large woodpecker that
hunts for bugs in old trees,
the Red-Bellied Woodpecker
is known to store its food in
cracks in trees for later.

**Nuthatch**—This is the
only bird that can walk
up and down a tree
headfirst, and indeed,
it is usually seen upside
down as it searches for
food. One of the only
birds to use tools. They
often use bark or sticks
to pry up bark while
looking for insects.

59

**Turkey Vulture**—Unlike other birds, turkey vultures have a great sense of smell. These "garbage collectors" can smell dead things from over a mile away! Their heads are bare to keep them clean as they eat. If bothered, they throw up on their harassers in order to escape!

**Bald Eagle**—The U.S. national symbol and arguably the most famous bird in the country, the Bald Eagle is a species we almost lost. The Bald Eagle was severely endangered in the 1970s, but its populations have recovered well thanks to laws that helped protect the environment and banned chemicals (such as DDT) that were hurting eagles.

Eagles are opportunistic hunters; they will often steal food from other birds. They can have a wingspan of up to 7½ feet!

**Red-Tailed Hawk**—The most common hawk in the USA, as well as one of the largest. They have a very distinctive reddish-brown tail. Their eyesight is incredible, and they can spot prey from high off the ground!

**Sharp-Shinned Hawk**—These small hawks have long legs, short wings and long tails: which they use to help them fly fast through the trees after their prey. They are sometimes seen by bird feeders because that is their primary prey. Females are about a third larger than males (a big size difference)!

**Great Horned Owl**—Those "ears" are actually feathers (not horns), and they may help with hearing by deflecting sound. These owls have a terrible sense of smell, so they enjoy eating skunks, but they have excellent eyesight! And like most owls, this one has fringed, soft feathers that muffle sound.

**Barn Owl**—This bird is becoming rarer endangered as it loses its habitat. They have heart-shaped, dishlike faces to funnel sound. Like other owls, they swallow their food whole and then spit out the bones and fur in what's called a "pellet." Gross, but cool!

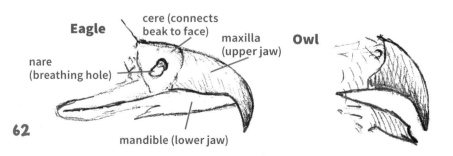

Eagle

cere (connects beak to face)

nare (breathing hole)

maxilla (upper jaw)

Owl

mandible (lower jaw)

**Screech Owl**—These neat owls have two different color patterns: gray or reddish brown. Both colors blend into the woods, providing excellent camouflage.

**Kestrel**—This is North America's smallest falcon. It is slightly larger than a robin, but has bright colors. They sometimes hover as they hunt for their prey, usually bugs or small mammals.

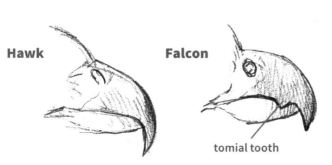

**Hawk**   **Falcon**

tomial tooth

Falcons have a special notch on their beaks called a tomial tooth. It is sort of like the edge of a knife, and it helps them kill their prey.

63

**Canada Goose**—A common goose now, but due to overhunting, they were almost extinct not that long ago. They can be very territorial, so give them space. Geese fly in a "V" formation; they take turns at the front, where it's hardest to fly, and flying behind a bird makes flying more efficient and easier. They fly as a team!

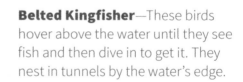

**Belted Kingfisher**—These birds hover above the water until they see fish and then dive in to get it. They nest in tunnels by the water's edge.

**Did you Know?** Kingfishers dive fast for their prey in the water (up to 25 miles per hour!), but even cooler are their beaks: they are really long for that size bird, hard, and sharp. They kind of slice into the water, creating no sound! The designers of Japanese bullet trains (the really fast ones) studied the aerodynamics of the kingfisher's beak to design the front of their trains to prevent sonic boom going through tunnels!

**Mallard Duck**—The most common and widespread duck in North America, the male is famous for its green head, brown front, and curled tail. Females are more brownish. They have a special gland that helps keep their feathers waterproof.

**Swan**—A beautiful bird to see floating on a pond, but keep your distance: Swans, like geese, can be territorial and protective of their nests. They are also huge: their wingspan can be up to seven feet!

**Great Blue Heron**—You will almost always find these birds standing very still at the water's edge, hunting. They stand very still when they see their prey, and then strike fast with their long necks and beaks. They'll even eat large fish, like Northern Pike!

**Did you Know?** Most ducks can hold their breath underwater for about a minute, but loons can stay underwater for five minutes!

**Common Loon**—Swimming and diving birds with long bodies and red eyes, loons have solid bones, unlike other birds, which helps them sink in the water as they dive. Loons have a variety of calls. Some sound like laughter, while others sound a bit eerie—and which you can often hear as sound effects in movies.

**Red-Winged Blackbird**— You will usually find these birds along the roadside ditches or near marshy ponds along the edge. The males have the flashiest feathers, while the females blend in with brown markings. They are one of the most common birds in North America!

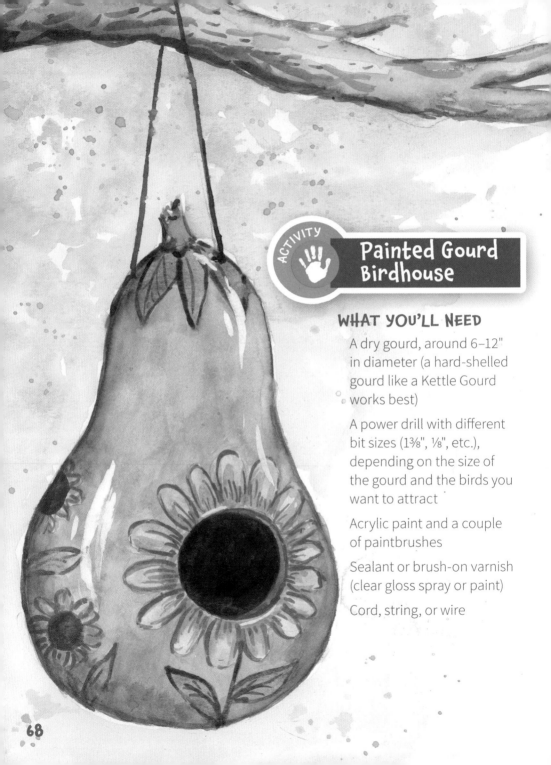

## Painted Gourd Birdhouse

### WHAT YOU'LL NEED

A dry gourd, around 6–12" in diameter (a hard-shelled gourd like a Kettle Gourd works best)

A power drill with different bit sizes (1⅜", ⅛", etc.), depending on the size of the gourd and the birds you want to attract

Acrylic paint and a couple of paintbrushes

Sealant or brush-on varnish (clear gloss spray or paint)

Cord, string, or wire

1. If you have grown your own gourd, make sure it is completely dry. It takes 2–3 months to dry out if you are growing your own. Have an adult help you use the larger drill bit to drill an entrance hole in the side (wear a mask for the dust!). Scoop out the insides, and clean the gourd as much as you can.

2. Use the small drill bit to drill two holes at the top to hang it, and two or three near the bottom for drainage.

3. Paint your gourd! You might want to paint a white base coat first so your colors show up brightly. You can also leave it natural colors to let it blend in. Be creative!

4. Spray or brush with two layers of varnish and let dry completely.

5. Use either a string or a wire to hang it up in a safe space in your yard!

Tip: Take it down and store it over the winter so it lasts longer. Note: If your gourd is really rough, you can sand it lightly before painting.

## ACTIVITY

# Pinecone Snowy Owl

## WHAT YOU'LL NEED

Pinecones (round and not-too-large ones work best)

Cotton balls

Felt, yellow, black, and white

Black permanent marker (Sharpie)

Plastic googly eyes

Hot glue gun

1. "Stuff" your pinecone! First fluff up your cotton balls: Pull them apart until they are fluffy. Then shove little pieces into the spaces of the pinecone. You can shove bits in with the back end of a pencil or a paintbrush if that helps. Stuff it in everywhere until full!

2. Cut your felt: For the wings, stack the felt so you can cut two wings at the same time and the same size (or trace the first onto the second). Use a black Sharpie to add the black markings on the wings.

**3** For the eyes, cut the yellow felt to be slightly larger than the plastic googly eyes, and glue the googly eyes to the felt you cut out. Cut a long diamond shape out of the black felt for the beak.

**4** Glue it all together!

Tip: Glue the felt directly to the pinecone (or the cotton can just pull off).

Another tip: If your pinecone doesn't sit straight upright, you can glue your owl to a small cardboard square.

American Toad

Fowler's Toad

# Amphibians and Reptiles

## TOADS

Toads have cool ways to be unappetizing to predators: Their warts produce a poison that tastes bad. Happily, it's not dangerous to humans. When threatened, they also urinate (pee!) on themselves to taste nasty, and they can inflate their bodies to look harder to eat. And rest assured, you won't get warts from touching a toad. That's a myth.

They are great for gardens because they eat lots of insects.

They hibernate by digging down into the dirt or piles of leaves for the winter. They then slow their bodies down to survive.

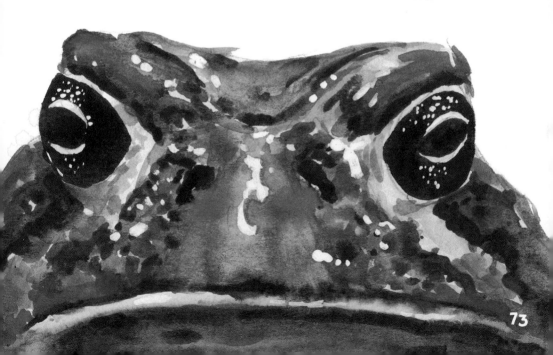

**American Bullfrog**

## FROGS

Frogs have excellent night vision. And because their eyes bulge out so far, they have a huge range of vision: up, down, and side to side.

Frogs drink water through their skin! Some even have a special "drinking patch" to absorb water.

There are more than 5,000 species of frogs around the world, and they live on every continent except Antarctica.

A frog's ear is called a tympanum; it's the circle behind the eye. Frogs communicate by songs, so it's not surprising they have good hearing!

Frogs, toads, salamanders, and newts are all amphibians: This means they spend part of their life on land, and part in the water. Frogs are born as eggs laid in the water, which hatch into tadpoles. Young tadpoles are a lot like fish; they swim with their tails and use gills to get oxygen. As they grow legs and lungs, they move out of the water onto land.

Northern
Leopard Frog

Gray Treefrog

## SALAMANDERS, LIZARDS, AND MORE

Salamanders are nocturnal, but you might find one under a rotten log. If you do find one, don't handle them, as your skin (or chemicals on it) can dry them out or hurt them. You can put them on a damp paper towel to look closer at them!

**Fun Fact:**
Salamanders can also regrow lost limbs: legs, feet, and tails.

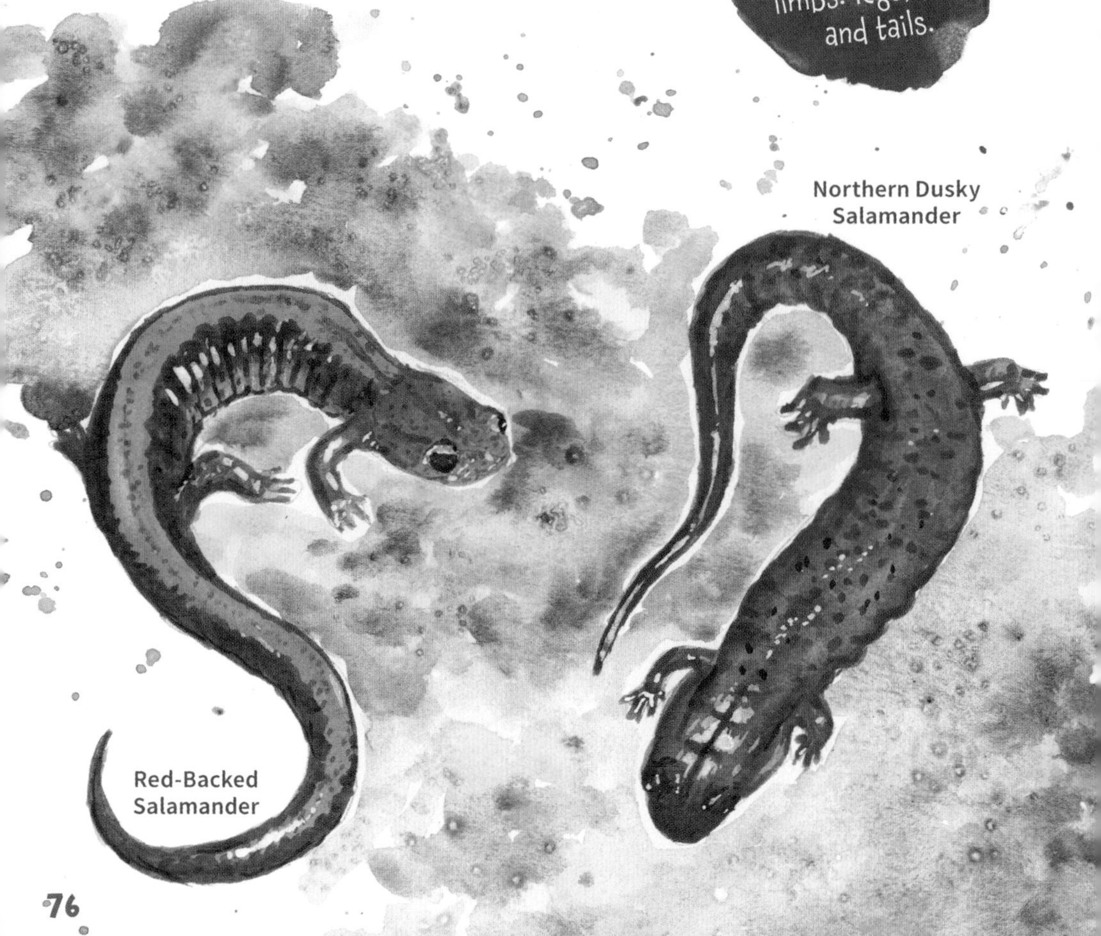

Northern Dusky Salamander

Red-Backed Salamander

**Five-Lined Skink**—These lizards are really amazing! Females and juveniles have bright-bluish-purple tails, and the males eventually turn brown as they get older. Like most lizards, they can lose their tails without being injured: The tail tip flops around and looks alive, distracting the predator. The skink can then regrow their tail later.

The Five-Lined Skink is one of the more common lizards in the U.S. Even though it looks like a salamander, a skink is a reptile, a different group of animals. Salamanders are more closely related to frogs than lizards.

## SNAKES

**Garter snakes** are common, harmless snakes that are helpful to have around—they eat small rodents and bugs. When scared they can give off a musky smell. Like all snakes, they swallow their prey whole, and hibernate in the winter. Garter snakes give birth to between 10 and 40 live baby snakes (not eggs!) that are immediately able to live on their own.

**Rat snakes** are also harmless. As their name suggests, they love to eat rats. They are also constrictors, squeezing their prey to death, just like the famous boa constrictors do.

Garter Snake

Eastern Black Rat Snake

# Turtles and Fish

Fish are cold-blooded (like turtles). They have no eyelids! And fish breathe through their gills (they have no lungs).

**Painted Turtles** are some of the most common turtles found in North America. They get their name because they appear "painted" with bright-yellow and orange markings.

Yellow Perch

**Did You Know?** A turtle's shell isn't just a shell they live in; it's their body, and it's made of bone.

Smallmouth Bass

Turtles survive the winter beneath the ice; they hibernate all winter at the bottom of lakes and ponds. Their bodies slow down a lot, and then they breathe—this is no joke—through their butts. (The techni-term is cloacal breathing, and it provides enough oxygen for them to survive.)

**Painted Turtle**

**Sunfish**

**Crayfish**

# Mammals

**Squirrels** are creative and clever: They store their food up for the winter, and they can even smell food when it's covered in snow! Sometimes, you might see a gray squirrel with all-black fur. These aren't a different species; instead, they are a color variety produced by a genetic mutation (an error in the squirrel's genetic code). There are all-white (leucistic) squirrels too!

Red Squirrel

Gray Squirrel

Flying Squirrel

**Flying squirrels** are much smaller, very shy, and nocturnal. They glide instead of fly, thanks to a long skin flap that stretches from wrist to ankle. Flying squirrels have huge eyes, too, perfect for seeing at night!

**Chipmunk**

**Chipmunks** are the smallest members of the squirrel family. They mostly live on the ground or beneath it, but they can climb trees too.

**Opossums** are North America's only marsupial, a special group of mammals most famous (like the kangaroo) for carrying their young in a pouch. Opossums do this too! They are also famous for hissing when threatened and then playing dead—convincingly—by rolling on their back, going limp, and sticking their tongue out, cartoon-style. (They'll also release a nasty odor to make themselves less appealing.)

**Eastern Cottontail Rabbit**

**Virginia Opossum**

A **rabbit**'s big ears aren't just for hearing. They also help regulate body temperature. Rabbits can't sweat, so they pant (like dogs) and lose heat through their ears. A rabbit's eyes are located on the sides of its head, helping them see in lots of different directions. This makes it hard for predators to sneak up on them.

83

Coyote

**Coyotes** are a common resident in cities and rural areas alike. Even big cities like Chicago have resident coyote populations! They are omnivores—meaning they eat plants *and* other animals—but they aren't much of a threat to people. You might hear coyotes talking to each other at night—they howl, bark, and yip.

**Foxes** are mostly solitary animals, unlike wolves, which often live in packs. They have vertical eye slits, like a cat, to help them see better at night. They are somewhat doglike and can be curious and playful, but they can also be quite timid and shy. And to answer that famous question—What does the fox say?—they make a loud, awful scream!

**Skunks** are unique critters. They are boldly colored, and they make little attempt to hide from other animals. Instead, they let their black-and-white coloration and obvious stinky smell convince predators to stay away. It works! They only spray when they are scared, but that spray is impressive: They can spray up to 10 feet in the air, have pinpoint accuracy, and the spray can be detected from a mile and a half away! When really threatened, they can adjust their spray and aim for the eyes, which causes temporary blindness. Spraying is a last resort, and they will first try to warn the threat away by stamping their feet, raising their tail, and dancing around.

Striped
Skunk

Red Fox

**Beavers** are the largest rodents in North America. They are one of the only animals that change their habitat on purpose. This, in turn, creates habitats for other animals. A beaver's orange teeth grow constantly; this is important, as the teeth wear down as the beaver chews down trees. Believe it or not, young beavers sound like human babies as they cry or talk to their parents.

A male **deer** is called a buck, a female deer is a doe, and a baby deer is called a fawn. Fawns are covered with spots, which helps them hide when their mother leaves them for short periods of time to forage. If you see a fawn alone in the woods, it's OK—leave it alone. Its mother will be coming back for it soon. Adult male deer grow new antlers every spring and shed (or lose) them every winter. It can really fun to go "shed hunting" to find old antlers!

White-Tailed
Deer

# Animal Tracks

**1. Who am I?** A nocturnal, clever creature known for its very human-like hands and "mischievous" behavior!

**2. Who am I?** When I run, my toes spread out and sometimes you see my dew claws, which show up like two dots. I can run up to 30 miles an hour.

**3. Who am I?** I am a marsupial and carry my babies in my pouch or clinging to my back. My tracks look kind of like a little kids' handprints.

**4. Who am I?** My tracks are usually around two feet apart. When I am happy, I sometimes jump in the air and kick my feet around.

*1. Northern Raccoon; 2. White-Tailed Deer; 3. Opossum; 4. Cottontail Rabbit*

**5. Who am I?** A playful and shy backyard nighttime visitor, this creature can make over 40 different sounds! They can be shy and hide, or curious and inquisitive.

**6. Who am I?** My tail helps me balance and keeps me warm. I flick it when I'm startled or alarmed.

**8. Who am I?** A clever and curious creature who loves to explore the world around me!

**7. Who am I?** I have very good eyesight, and I'm quite clever. I sleep in trees at night, and can run almost 20 miles an hour.

# Wilder Creatures

You might not get a chance to see these, but keep your eyes open and be really quiet, and someday you might! Of course, always be careful in the woods, especially with our wilder friends. Remember that all animals are wild and unpredictable.

**American Badger**

**Pine Marten**

**Least Weasel**

**Fisher**

**Weasels**—North America has many cool creatures in the weasel family (Mustelidae) if you are lucky enough to see them! Most of them are very fast, shy, and elusive. Examples include the American Marten and the tiny Least Weasel, along with River Otters, Fishers, and Minks. Most mustelids have long bodies and powerful feet for digging, fishing, and catching their prey—they are all carnivores.

**River Otter**

**Black Bear**—If you see one in the wild, stay calm and keep your distance. Never try to feed a bear or touch it, and tell an adult immediately if you see a bear.

# Butterflies and Bugs

Monarch

**How a monarch caterpillar turns into an adult butterfly**

**Monarch Butterflies** journey from the Great Lakes and the northern U.S. to Mexico (or California), a distance of about 3,000 miles, and return to the north again in the spring. They have recently been listed as endangered by the International Union for Conservation of Nature, and they may be listed as endangered by the U.S. government as well. Their favorite plants, which they depend upon for survival, are milkweeds.

A butterfly goes through three stages before it is fully grown: egg, larva (caterpillar), and pupa (chrysalis). A caterpillar goes through a number of molting phases as it grows. These phases are called "instars"; with each one, the caterpillar gets bigger. Eventually, the caterpillar finds a suitable location, attaches a sturdy silk pad to the underside, and develops into a chrysalis. Inside the chrysalis, the caterpillar transforms into an adult. For example, a Monarch will spend 8–15 days as a chrysalis before crawling out as a crumpled and wet butterfly. It will need to dry and strengthen its wings before it can fly.

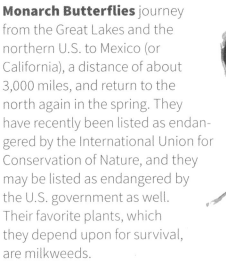

Question Mark

Tiger Swallowtail

**Black Swallowtail**

Antarctica is the only continent on which no butterflies or moths have been found.

Butterflies can see in color, and they also see ultraviolet light (which human eyes can't see).

Cabbage White
(invasive)

Painted Lady

Buckeye

**Did You Know?** The Cabbage White Butterfly is one of the most common butterflies in many places in North America, but it's an invasive species
(an introduced species that does major damage to the environment).
It feeds on a huge variety of plants (including garden plants, such as
cabbage, which is where it gets its name). It has spread onto every
continent except South America and Antarctica.

Banded
Sphinx Moth

Luna Moth

## MOTHS

What is the difference between butterflies and moths? Here are a few tips: Butterflies are usually only found during the day, but some moths are active during the day too. Hummingbird moths, which get their name because they are often mistaken for hummingbirds, visit flowers during the day and are fun to watch. They hover at flowers, drinking nectar by using their long, coiled tongue.

Butterflies usually have antennae that are club shaped. A moth's antennae look more feathery or fernlike.

Butterflies often usually fold their wings up when they rest. Moths are generally more nocturnal and they also tend to fold their wings out flat when they rest (to blend in with their backgrounds). Moth bodies are generally more stocky, and fuzzy, and their antennae are more feathery.

Luna moths are large, beautiful moths that only come out at night and live as adults for about a week. They don't even have mouths and don't eat as adults! But they eat a lot as a large, hungry caterpillar.

**Common Gray Moth**

**Hummingbird Sphinx Moth**

Grasshopper

Insects are invertebrates. They don't have bones. Instead, they have what's called an exoskeleton on the outside of their bodies. This tough covering protects the insect and helps them retain water so they don't dry out.

A **grasshopper**'s ears are near its belly! They use their ears to listen to other grasshopper calls and to detect predators. Their jumping ability is impressive. A grasshopper is maybe 2 inches long, but they can jump up to 30 inches. If you could jump like a grasshopper, you could jump something like 60 feet! (That's the length of a basketball court!)

The **Praying Mantis** is an impressive hunter! It ambushes its prey, jumping and striking at lightning speed. But it has many other extreme adaptations. It sees in 3D vision—this means it has depth perception—and not only that, this special ability only works on something that's moving (like their prey!). A Praying Mantis is also the only insect that can turn its head.

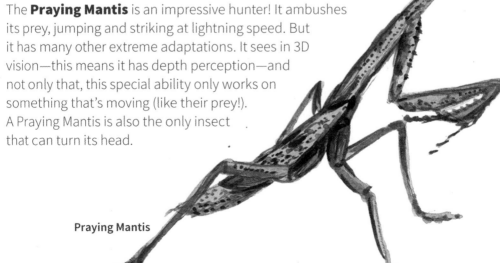

Praying Mantis

**Walking sticks** are masters of disguise. They are hard to find or see because of how much they resemble sticks! Some other cool facts about walking stick insects: They can shed a leg if threatened, and then regrow it! They also "play dead," falling to the ground and lying still, like a fallen twig. Even their eggs are camouflaged and look like seeds!

**Dragonflies** start their lives out in water, where they live for almost 2 years, eating anything they can find. Then they crawl out, their exoskeleton cracks open, and their wings come out! They catch their prey while flying (including many mosquitoes), and they can fly forward, back, up, and down, and they can even hover!

Walking Stick

Blue Dasher
Dragonfly

**Ladybugs** are sweet little garden visitors, but did you know they aren't actually a bug? Entomologists (people who study insects) group bugs into families, and ladybugs are actually beetles. Sometimes called ladybird beetles, they are a gardener's friend, as they eat lots of pest bugs, such as aphids. Unfortunately, there is an invasive ladybug that is now found in many places. It looks like our native ones, but it has an annoying habit of entering homes and hanging out on the outside walls of houses and buildings.

Ladybug

You'll often hear **crickets** chirping in your backyard. Those are the males calling females (and keeping other males away). They have many different songs they can "sing," and each species has a unique song as well.

**Cricket**

**Dog Day Cicada**

**Cicadas** are another noisy backyard friend! These big bugs—they belong to the true bug family of insects—are usually seen during the long days (the "dog days") of summer when it is really hot. They make a loud, sirenlike whine that lasts about 15 seconds, getting louder and louder, then dropping off at the end. You might find a brown, dried-up "shell" of a young cicada. This was left behind when a nymph became an adult cicada on a tree or your house. The papery husks are fun to find, so take a look!

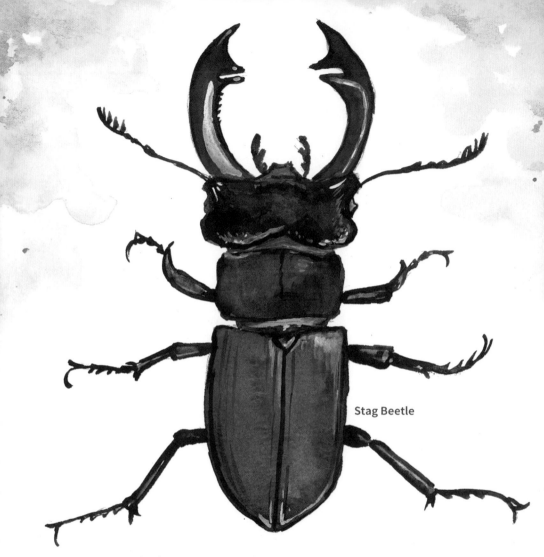

Stag Beetle

Beetles have two sets of wings: the first set consists of hardened wing cases called elytra. These act kind of like body armor. The back two are used to fly.

**June Beetle (or May/June Bug)**—Most often seen during early-to-mid summer, and especially the months of May and June. June beetles are harmless to people but can be a pest for farmers. They are most active at night, but you might find them bumbling around near lights.

> "I love to think of nature as an unlimited broadcasting station, through which God speaks to us every hour if we will only tune in."
>
> George Washington Carver

**Firefly**—These fun bugs show up at twilight, and they light up! A firefly has a special "lantern organ" in its abdomen. Its body creates a special chemical that helps its lantern light up! Animals that can make light are called bioluminescent. Fireflies have their own blinking patterns (just like bird calls) to attract mates. They also want to let other animals know that they taste really bad! Even firefly eggs and larvae glow!

**June Beetle
(or May/June Bug)**

Firefly

# ROLY-POLY, ACORN RAMSHEAD SNAIL, WHIRLIGIG BEETLE

These bugs are going around in circles! Roly-Poly bugs (also known as pill-bugs) are isopods. Isopods are actually crustaceans, not insects, and are related to lobsters and crabs! Pillbugs live on land, and they can roll up into perfectly round balls. They have seven sets of legs and a shell that segments like a lobster tail. They curl up when threatened and their shell acts like armor. They make great pets!

**Snails**—There are a lot of invasive snails around, so get to know your area's native species! Snails are mollusks, a group of animals that includes snails, slugs, clams, and even octopus and squids. This snail is small—about a half inch or smaller. The spiral of a snail's shell shows up in nature often–think of the spiral of flower petals or the shape of a pinecone. Look around your yard for a naturally occurring spiral!

Acorn Ramshorn Snail

Roly-Poly

**Whirligig Beetle**—These water beetles spin and swirl on the surface of the water and can dive under if they feel threatened. They have two sets of eyes, so they can see above and below the water at the same time!

## BEES, WASPS, AND MORE

Bees, hornets, wasps, and ants talk to each other using a complex system of pheromones—chemicals they can sense in the air—to communicate about threats or food sources. Honeybees can even accurately give direction to a food source. They do this in a surprising way: They dance. This "waggle dance" (which looks like a figure eight) was recently decoded, and it uses the sun as a reference point, and the bee's dance moves as directions!

Honeybee

Bumblebee

Yellowjacket

Wasp

**Bees**—Bees are great natural pollinators! About 90 percent of native plants need bees to pollinate them! Most depend on native bees—not honeybees, which are basically farm animals. This makes native bees really important, and better yet, most aren't aggressive at all. (Instead, they are fun backyard visitors.) So do your part to help our native bees: Plant lots of native flowering plants for them in your backyard, and avoid using nasty yard chemicals and pesticides. You will love all the extra bees, butterflies, and even birds that you start seeing!

**Yellowjacket**—A guest that often invites itself to picnics, these wasps aren't bees (though they are often referred to as one). They can sometimes be aggressive, especially if their nest is disturbed or they feel threatened. They can nest in hollow spaces (like logs or tree stumps) or in the ground, in colonies of up to 5,000 individuals!

# Maple Seed Dragonflies

## WHAT YOU'LL NEED

Craft paper or wax paper

Craft paint (acrylic) and brushes

Maple seeds (available at garden stores if there aren't any maple trees nearby)

Hot glue

Twigs (small, skinny, and straight ones)

1. Lay out some scrap paper or wax paper to cover your table. Then start to paint your maple seeds. Have fun with your colors—any combinations will work! Let them dry.

2. Glue your maple seeds together. Have an adult help you with the hot glue! Glue a smaller set of "wings" onto a bigger set. Layer them one on top of the other, as shown in the illustrations.

3. Cut your little twigs into pieces about 2–3" long. Glue the twig onto the wings so that the end is longer on one side.

4. If the stems stick out far from your maple seeds, trim them to look like antennae.

You can do so much with these! Glue them onto a wire and put in a flowerpot. Attach to fishing line of varying lengths, and make a mobile to fly in the wind. Use them to decorate a present or table setting.

# Put Out a Moth Light!

## WHAT YOU'LL NEED

A light-colored sheet

String/cord/clothespins or clips

A bright flashlight

Tip: If you want more moths, try a short-wavelength UV light (also known as a black light); you will get a wider variety of moths and other bugs. These are available online.

Let's explore our nighttime friends! This activity works best on a warm summer night without too much of a breeze.

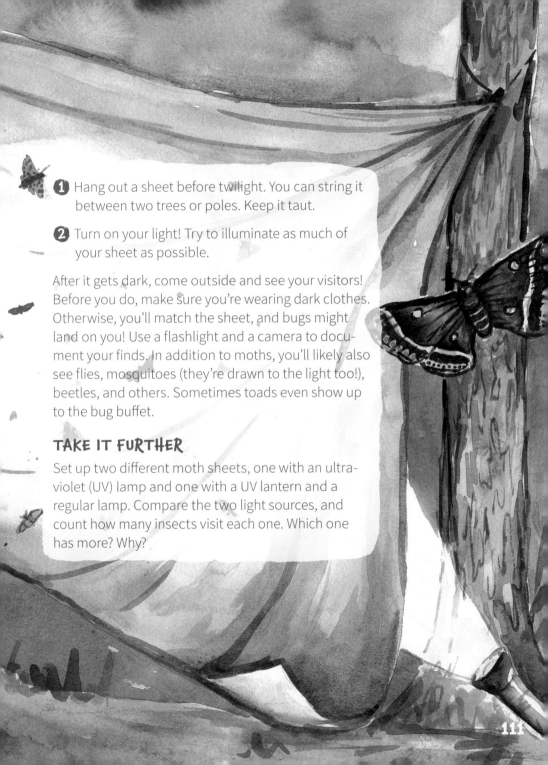

1. Hang out a sheet before twilight. You can string it between two trees or poles. Keep it taut.

2. Turn on your light! Try to illuminate as much of your sheet as possible.

After it gets dark, come outside and see your visitors! Before you do, make sure you're wearing dark clothes. Otherwise, you'll match the sheet, and bugs might land on you! Use a flashlight and a camera to document your finds. In addition to moths, you'll likely also see flies, mosquitoes (they're drawn to the light too!), beetles, and others. Sometimes toads even show up to the bug buffet.

## TAKE IT FURTHER

Set up two different moth sheets, one with an ultraviolet (UV) lamp and one with a UV lantern and a regular lamp. Compare the two light sources, and count how many insects visit each one. Which one has more? Why?

111

# Moss and Lichen

There's a whole little world right outside your door! Crouch down and sit still, and look close at moss and lichen! Take your time exploring, maybe use a magnifying glass. Pretend you are tiny and walking through this little world: What would you see? What would it be like? Where would you live? Use your imagination.

Mosses are plants. Typically, moss needs moisture, so it is more common in areas where the ground stays pretty damp. Moss doesn't usually grow very tall, and it doesn't really have a root system, so try not to disturb much of it. (It takes a long time to grow.) What kinds of moss do you see? There are so many different kinds!

Lichen looks like moss, but it is its own unique thing. Moss is a plant, but lichen is actually more than one kind of life-form: It consists of algae or bacteria that lives with fungi. Moss has tiny leaves and stems, but lichen looks like flat plates or tiny tubes. Some lichens even grow on rocks!

**Mushrooms** are fungi, a group of organisms that are totally different from plants and animals. The mushroom that you see on the grass or growing on wood is a bit like a mushroom's "fruit." The actual fungus is below, in the soil or within the wood. You'll see it as thin threads; that's called the mycelium.

Note: Let wild mushrooms stay wild, and simply enjoy spotting them and snapping photos! (Hint: Many mushrooms are the perfect size for posing a Lego minifigure or a plastic dino underneath.)

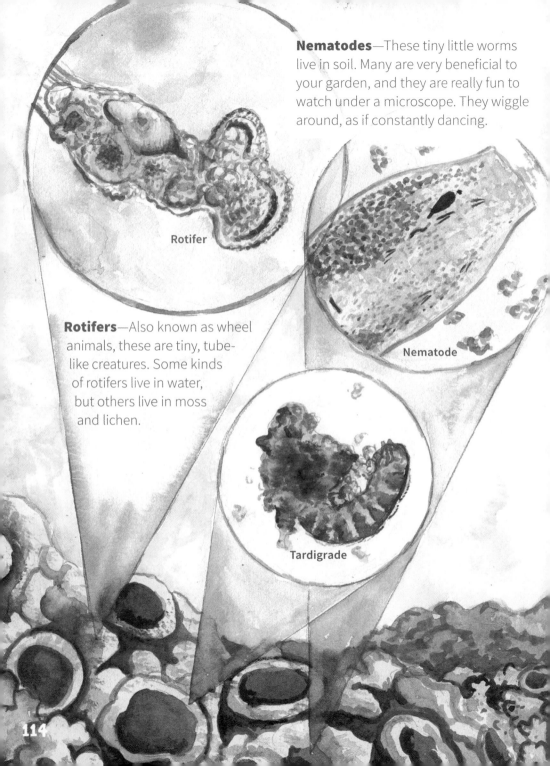

**Nematodes**—These tiny little worms live in soil. Many are very beneficial to your garden, and they are really fun to watch under a microscope. They wiggle around, as if constantly dancing.

Rotifer

Nematode

**Rotifers**—Also known as wheel animals, these are tiny, tube-like creatures. Some kinds of rotifers live in water, but others live in moss and lichen.

Tardigrade

# THE MICRO WORLD

Let's look even closer! If you were to take a microscope and look closer at some moss or lichen, you would see a whole new world. A tiny, tiny world! In fact, there are lots of little creatures bustling around and living their lives right "under our noses." Every bit of moss you see is actually a mini city, teeming with unique and diverse creatures. Here are a few residents visible under a microscope.

Tardigrade

**Tardigrades**—Also known as Water Bears or Moss Piglets, these are are truly darling tiny creatures that live in moss, lichen, in lakes/rivers, and pretty much everywhere between. They have eight legs, impressive claws, eyes, a brain, and a mouth, and a stomach. (They're also usually invisible without a microscope.) Weirder yet, they are tough little critters. When conditions aren't good, tardigrades can go into what's called a "tun" state. They shrivel up into a little ball, and their bodies slow down to a stop (almost like a big pause button). When they are in a "tun" state, they can survive almost anything: freezing, boiling, poisonous gases, and even outer space itself. Even though they are pretty easy to find, the wildest part is this: in some states they haven't been studied much at all! So get tardigrade hunting and you could contribute to real science!

# How to Draw

## BIRDS

**1** Find the basic shapes! Most birds are two shapes: a circle for the head and an oval for the body. Ask yourself: How long is the body compared to the head? You can use the end of your pencil to measure. Draw lightly!

**2** Sketch the rest of the basic body parts: neck, tail (keep it simple still: just a triangle), beak, eye, and the angle of the legs.

**3** Details! Now you get to add all the amazing features birds have. Look closely! Notice that the beak extends into the face, almost to the eye! Notice that bird eyes do not show any whites of the eye, like humans do. Bird eyes are very rounded, not football shaped. Also notice how bird feet grip the branch. They don't stand up tall on their tippy toes; their feet grab what they are standing on. Notice different length feathers on their wings—they end in rows. At this point, you can erase your original circles.

If you want to, use your pencil to shade, or colored pencils or paint to color. Notice that bird feathers grow down, away from the head, so color in that direction in little short strokes to look like real feather texture.

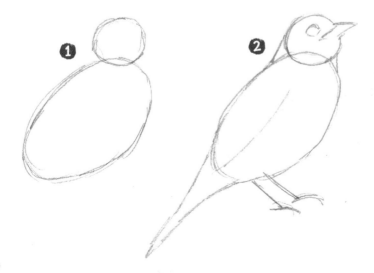

③

# How to Draw

## TOADS

**1** Find the basic shapes! Toads have no neck, so the body (circle) and head (oval) overlap a lot! Use the end of your pencil to measure the sizes and get the proportions right.

**2** Sketch the rest of the body parts. For the back legs, start with an oval, then draw the "S" shape of the bent leg. Find the front legs, eyes, and tympanum (ear) and the big bump behind the eyes. The arms extend into the body.

**3** Details! Add warts and markings! Check out a toad's eye—the pupils are oval or football shaped! Notice the texture and the angle of the toad's back.

If you want to, use your pencil to shade darks and lights. If you want to color it in, maybe start with a light tan, and then layer the dark spots and bumps.

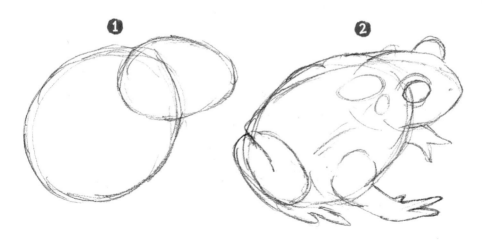

# How to Draw

## BLACK BEAR

**1** Find the basic shapes! This bear is quite round—both its body and its head! Check the proportions to make sure you get your shapes the right size.

**2** Sketch the rest of the bear's body. Connect the head to the body to create a wide neck. Artists sometimes use a **+** shape over a face to help them place the facial features—in this case, the **+** is turned to the side, making its face look to the side. The eyes are usually about halfway down the face. The legs are quite wide and connect to the outside of the bear's body. Notice the angles of the ears and legs; you can rest you pencil on the page to see what angle they are. Notice how the bear's muzzle sticks out past the **+** to look 3D.

**3** Details! Check out the claws and his nose: Leave the top a little lighter. Notice how small a bear's eyes are in proportion to its face.

**Shade or color**—Even an all-black bear isn't just black! Look for the highlights (lighter areas), and make the shadowed areas much darker to help the bear look 3D. Also, be aware that black animals often have shades of blue or brown or purple to their fur.

# How to Draw

## BUTTERFLY

**1** Find the basic shapes! Butterfly wings are made of two shapes: The front wing is often a triangle, and the bottom wing is a teardrop shape. Notice that the triangle curves out on the top. The wing shapes extend far out above the body. (And notice how small the body is!)

**2** Round the corners of the triangle, and bring the edge in. Give the butterfly a head shape, antennae, and a tail.

**3** Details! Start to break up the wing into the different shapes. Start with the simplified main shapes (on the left side), and then add in the veins (on the right side).

**Shade or color**—Notice the white spots: Shade around them! If you are coloring, it is easiest to just color orange over most of the wing first (not the edge), then draw the black over it. Try to make the two sides look as much alike as you can!

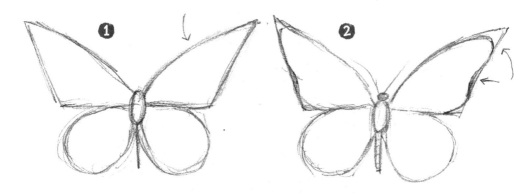

③

# How to Draw

## SQUIRREL

**1** Find the basic shapes! Squirrels are very round! Use your pencil to measure the size of the head compared to the body.

**2** Sketch in the rest of the body—keep it simple! Attach the head to the body with its neck, and find the curves of the legs. Keep the hands/feet to just ovals to work on the right size. The eye is close to the middle of the face.

**3** Details! Notice the fingers and toes! A squirrel's nose looks different from your dog or cat's nose. Notice the squirrel's eye is a very rounded football shape.

**Shade or color**—Notice the direction of a squirrel's fur: It grows away from the head on the body. Use short lines to represent the texture of fur. On the tail, the lines curve up and back around the top—keep these lines longer. If you are coloring, you will want to layer grays and browns. Don't forget whiskers!

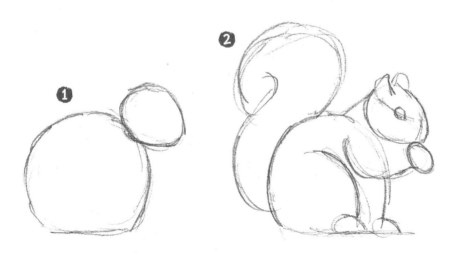

③

# How to Draw

## FLOWERS

**1** Draw basic shapes! Decide what shape of flower you want to draw: An oval? Ignore the petals until you have the basic outside shape—this will help your flower stay even. Sketch the center of your flower—is it an oval or a cone? Or maybe it isn't visible!

**2** How many petals does your flower have? Draw a line out from the center for each petal to space them out (draw this lightly!).

**3** Sketch the petal shapes. Notice that if a petal is closer to you, it is larger and might fold over. Look at what you actually see, not what you think you see (a symbol). Do the petals overlap? Do they curl over?

## TIPS

If you are drawing a bouquet, it's usually easier to draw the flowers first, then fill in the leaves and stems around them after. Overlap shapes to make the bouquet have depth. Let some leaves be sideways or curled to make the flowers look more real.

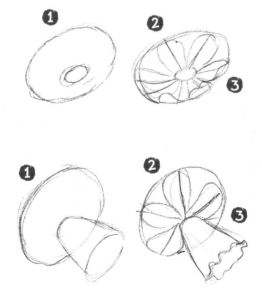

127

# Rock Collecting

Become a rockhound (someone who loves rocks and has a collection). You can use an old tackle box, jewelry box, or even an old egg carton to start your collection! Finding awesome rocks is like a treasure hunt—you never know what you will find!

First find out what rocks and minerals can be found in your area. *Important:* Also find out if you are allowed to take rocks from your location. Collecting at national parks and most state or local parks is against the law. Instead, just take photos.

If you start a rock collection, you should know the difference between rocks and minerals. Minerals are special combinations of chemicals that are unique. Examples include Lake Superior agates, quartz, calcite, garnet, salt, diamonds, and many others. There are many different kinds of minerals, and each is unique. Rocks are made up of two or more minerals. (That means granite, for example, consists of a whole bunch of different minerals.)

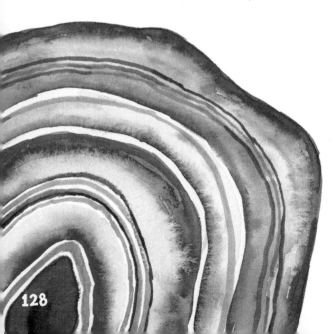

Petoskey Stone

Calcite

Limestone

Gneiss

Granite

Fluorite

Basalt

Blue Slagstone

Quartz

Jasper

**129**

# Rock Painting

Rock painting is such a fun activity with endless possibilities!

## WHAT YOU'LL NEED

  Scrap paper to cover your work area

  Acrylic paint, permanent markers (Sharpies), and paintbrushes

  Plastic googly eyes (optional)

  Outdoor acrylic sealer/acrylic spray varnish

**1** Collect smooth rocks, in whatever sizes you want. Wash and dry them.

**2** Lay down some scrap paper to protect your workspace.

**3** Paint a base color, one solid color that will be present under your patterns/image. Let it dry.

**4** Use paint and Sharpies to create patterns or animals! To paint dots, use a Q-tip or the back end of your paintbrush. Let dry. Glue googly eyes on animals if you like.

**5** Paint or spray an acrylic sealer on top to protect rocks from weather.

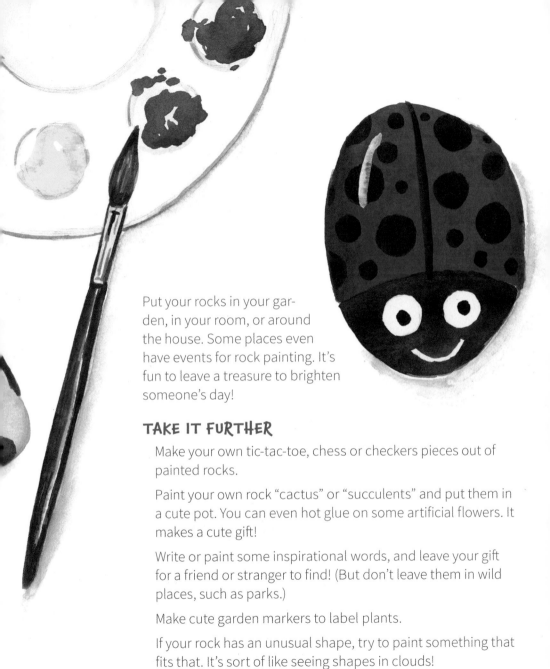

Put your rocks in your garden, in your room, or around the house. Some places even have events for rock painting. It's fun to leave a treasure to brighten someone's day!

## TAKE IT FURTHER

Make your own tic-tac-toe, chess or checkers pieces out of painted rocks.

Paint your own rock "cactus" or "succulents" and put them in a cute pot. You can even hot glue on some artificial flowers. It makes a cute gift!

Write or paint some inspirational words, and leave your gift for a friend or stranger to find! (But don't leave them in wild places, such as parks.)

Make cute garden markers to label plants.

If your rock has an unusual shape, try to paint something that fits that. It's sort of like seeing shapes in clouds!

# Recommended Reading

Andrews, Kim. *Exploring Nature Activity Book for Kids: 50 Creative Projects to Spark Curiosity in the Outdoors*. Rockridge Press, 2019.

Arment, Ainsley. *Wild and Free Nature: 25 Outdoor Adventures for Kids to Explore, Discover, and Awaken Their Curiosity*. HarperCollins, 2021.

Daniels, Jaret C. *Insects & Bugs Backyard Workbook: Hands-On Projects, Quizzes, and Activities*. Adventure Publications, 2021.

Hoare, Ben. *Nature's Treasures: Tales Of More Than 100 Extraordinary Objects From Nature*. Penguin Books, 2021.

Leslie, Clare Walker. *The Nature Connection: An Outdoor Workbook for Kids, Families, and Classrooms*. Storey Publishing, 2010.

Ortler, Brett. *Backyard Nature & Science Workbook: Midwest: Fun Activities & Experiments That Get Kids Outdoors*. Adventure Publications, 2021.

Storey Publishing, LLC. *Backpack Explorer: On the Nature Trail: What Will You Find?* 2018.

Rothman, Julia. *Nature Anatomy: The Curious Parts and Pieces of the Natural World*. Storey Publishing, LLC, 2015.

Zambello, Erika. *Backyard Birding for Kids: An Introduction to Ornithology*. Adventure Publications, 2022.

# Community Science

Kids can do real science too! Community science projects are a great way to get involved in real science wherever you are. Did you know that your pictures and notes about frogs, bugs, or the weather can actually help real scientists? They can! After all, there are far more regular people—and kids—than scientists, so by observing, photographing, and contributing your finds to online science projects, you can contribute to real science. Scientists regularly use these community science projects in scientific papers, research, and to help protect species!

There are so many ways you can participate in the science community.

Help the birds! Join the **Audubon Society's Christmas Bird Count** (www.audubon.org/conservation/science/christmas-bird-count), the **Celebrate Urban Birds Census** (https://celebrateurbanbirds.org), or the **Great American Bird Count** (www.birdcount.org). Keeping accurate numbers of our birds is one of the first things we can do to help them. All you need to do is watch and count! Or, this winter, help **Project FeederWatch** (https://feederwatch.org) record winter habits of backyard birds. For daily observations, **eBird** (https://ebird.org/home) allows you to upload photos daily of your sightings. Grab your binoculars and a camera!

Participate in a one-day butterfly count in your area through the **North America Butterfly Association** (www.naba.org/counts/participate.html), or help Monarch Butterflies directly by participating in the **Monarch Larva Monitoring Project** (https://monarchjointventure.org/mlmp).

**The National Phenology Network** (www.usanpn.org/usa-national-phenology-network) will help you learn about the plants in your area, while you observe and record what you see around you. **Project Budburst** (https://budburst.org) is an organization interested in monitoring plants and trees and how climate change is affecting them in your area.

And there's so much more: Ask your science teacher if they know of any other local groups or organizations that would love your help. And remember—caring about your environment starts with you, at home, with decisions you make about recycling, the plants in your yard, and how you go about protecting your planet.

# Glossary

**Amphibian** A group of animals that includes frogs and toads, newts, and salamanders; these animals spend their larval stage in water and their adult life on land.

**Beetle** Insects in the order Coleoptera; fireflies, ladybugs, and Junebugs are all beetles.

**Biological classification** A system that organizes all life-forms into related groups; levels are Kingdom, Phylum, Class, Order, Family, Genus, Species. Every life-form has exactly one name—a genus and a species—sort of like a first and last name. For example, domestic cats (house cats) belong to the kingdom Animalia (animals), the phylum Chordata (animals with a special nerve cord), the class Mammalia (mammals), the order Carnivora (carnivores), the family Felidae (cats), the genus *Felus* (small-to-medium cats), and the species name *catus*. That means your kitty's scientific name is *Felix catus*.

**Biologist** A scientist who studies living things.

**Bug** A generic name for any "creepy-crawly;" the word "bug" may also refer to insects belonging to the order Hemiptera, the true bugs.

**Chrysalis** A protective silk structure constructed by butterflies for their transition from a caterpillar to a butterfly.

**Cocoon** A protective silk structure made by moths for their transition from a caterpillar to a moth.

**Crop** A special pouch in the throat of some birds (doves, for example) that helps them store food to consume later.

**Cyanotype** Also known as a sun print, this is a special kind of photo printing that is great for preserving images of flowers, ferns, and more.

**Elytra** The hardened wing cases found on the front wings of beetles (the singular word is *elytron*).

**Entomologist** A scientist who studies insects.

**Evolution** The study of how life changes or evolves over time via natural selection.

**Fungi** A group of life-forms belonging to the kingdom Fungi. They often live in the soil or on trees, and when they fruit, some produce mushrooms.

**Habitat** Settings where animals, plants, and other life are found. Habitats are everywhere, from lush forests to suburban backyards.

**Insect** An animal belonging to the class Insecta; examples include beetles, bees, and butterflies and moths, among others. Common "creepy-crawlies" like spiders, ticks, and worms are not insects; they belong to different groups.

**Invertebrate**  An animal without a spinal cord.

**Isopod**  An order (see Biological classification) of crustaceans; many isopods live in the ocean, but some, such as pillbugs and wood lice, live on land.

**Larval stage**  The stage in an animal's life that follows the egg phase and occurs before adulthood. For example, caterpillars are the larval stage for butterflies.

**Leave No Trace**  Enjoying nature without leaving a trace of your presence once you're done. Don't leave trash, don't stack rocks, and take photos instead of keepsakes. See www.lnt.org for more information.

**Leucistic**  Describes an animal with a genetic mutation that makes its fur all-white (as in all-white squirrels).

**Lichen**  A group of life-forms that consist of fungi and bacteria that cooperate and live together. Lichen often live on tree bark and rocks.

**Marsupial**  A group of mammals that carry their young in a special pouch, which is found on the mother's belly. Examples include Virginia opossums, kangaroo, and wombats.

**Melanistic**  Describes an animal with an all-black coloration. Melanistic squirrels, for example, are solid black.

**Migration**  When animals move from one area to another. Seasonal bird migration is the most common example.

**Mineral**  A unique chemical compound that has solidified. Salt, for example, is a mineral and the combination of two chemicals: sodium and chlorine.

**Mollusk**  Animals in the phylum Mollusca, which includes slugs, snails, octopuses, and shelled animals such as clams.

**Mushroom**  The aboveground fruit of a fungus; mushrooms spread spores, which is how many mushrooms reproduce.

**Natural selection**  When a mutation (change) in a life-form helps it adapt, survive, and reproduce.

**Native bees**  Bee species that are native to a given area. Honeybees are not native bees, and most native bees don't live in large hives; instead, they live alone.

**Naturalist**  Someone who looks closely at nature: plants, animals, insects, fossils, and more.

**Nematode**  Wormlike animals that belong to the phylum Nematoda. They are often microscopic and, when viewed under a microscope, can often be seen wiggling around.

**Odonata**  An order of insects that includes dragonflies and damselflies.

**Pillbug**  An isopod that can roll itself up into a ball as a defense mechanism.

**Prism**  An object used to break light into its component colors.

**Rock**  A solid substance made up of minerals.

**Rotifer**  Microscopic, tubelike animals, often seen alongside tardigrades and nematodes.

**Shed**  Deer antlers that have been shed; sheds can be found in the spring.

**Tapetum lucidum**  A layer of mirrorlike cells in the eyes of certain animals, like dogs and cats, that help them see well in low-light conditions.

**Tardigrade**  A microscopic bearlike animal that lives in moss, lichen, and aquatic environments. Tardigrades are found everywhere on Earth and in their dormant state (called a tun) can survive in extreme conditions (boiling temperatures, strong radiation, even outer space).

**Terrarium**  A mini garden in a small space, often a closed glass container.